Praise for

Queers lik

❝ Michael V. Smith's *Queers Like Me* is a beautiful, funny, honest book. There were so many moments when I felt a loving kinship with Smith through queerness, through family, through home. Each page feels alive and so deeply human. This is a book to read and to be read through—a brilliant dive into belonging."

Jordan Abel
Griffin Poetry Prize–winning author of *Injun* and *NISHGA*

❝ Michael V. Smith is Canada's answer to Frank O'Hara. In poems at once charming in tone and yet devastating in subtext, rollicking in language and dignified in what is said as well as what remains unspoken, *Queers Like Me* explores the nature of family, place, and belonging from the perspective of a life lived on the artistic edge."

George Murray
author of *Problematica: New and Selected Poems*

❝ A verse memoir from several perspectives of identity, *Queers Like Me* is a faceted lexicon of Smith's experience of grief, desire, alienation, aging, and happiness. A warm, witty-tragic tale told in lineated conversational intimacy, with lines like 'I'm a bit emotionally barren / with some singing and dancing / thrown in,' this confessional/anti-confessional text feels like a friend you could talk to about anything."

Sharon Thesen
author of *The Wig-Maker*

Queers like me

poems   Michael V. Smith

poems

rs

ke me

Michael V. Smith

Book*hug Press
Toronto 2023

Library and Archives Canada Cataloguing in Publication
Title: Queers like me : poems / Michael V. Smith.
Names: Smith, Michael V., author.
Identifiers: Canadiana (print) 20230221505
            Canadiana (ebook) 20230221513
   ISBN 9781771668507 (softcover)
   ISBN 9781771668514 (EPUB)
   ISBN 9781771668521 (PDF)
Subjects: LCGFT: Poetry.
Classification: LCC PS8587.M5636 Q44 2023 | DDC C811/.6—dc23

The production of this book was made possible through the generous
assistance of the Canada Council for the Arts and the Ontario Arts
Council. Book*hug Press also acknowledges the support of the
Government of Canada through the Canada Book Fund and the
Government of Ontario through the Ontario Book Publishing Tax Credit
and the Ontario Book Fund.

Book*hug Press acknowledges that the land on which we operate is
the traditional territory of many nations, including the Mississaugas of
the Credit, the Anishnabeg, the Chippewa, the Haudenosaunee, and
the Wendat peoples. We recognize the enduring presence of many
diverse First Nations, Inuit, and Métis peoples and are grateful for the
opportunity to meet and work on this territory.

Book*hug Press

For Francis, my forever family

Contents

Grandma Cooper's Corpse

Here is how this story show
works:
  I have a Magic Story Bag
  and every day
  I draw a card
  with a title on it.

Today we drew...
     GRANDMA COOPER'S CORPSE

which is
a fucking
whopper
because it's hard to talk about
your grandmother's corpse

tho it *is* good
to learn new things.

  It doesn't matter how pretty you are,
  you always have more to learn cuz
  pretty doesn't last.
     [Michael taps forehead.]
  Brains do.

Grandma Cooper
was my mom's mom.

My extended family, both sides,
all live in a little tiny place within
a twenty-minute drive of each other.
Kemptville, Ontario.

      (We lived an hour away, in the city.)

Grandma Cooper
lived next to the beer store, so she knew
what was going on with the Smith side—
she could watch them
coming and going.
                      When I'd show up
at Grandma Cooper's, she'd say,
OH you know your grandfather
    —she meant my dad's dad—
your grandfather was at the beer store
yesterday AND today,
he got a two-four both times.

I knew my Smith grandparents'
drinking habits
because Grandma Cooper
paid attention.
Small town.

One day Dad phones
when I'm in Cornwall visiting my sister,
Mom is there too,
                    and Dad says
Are you sitting down?
I got some weird
news for you. Have you heard
about your Grandma Cooper?

And I'm like, No.

And he says, Well,
I think your Grandma Cooper is dead.

And I'm like, Oh fuck.

And he says, The story I heard from your uncle Ted
is that your uncle Bob got arrested
for transporting a corpse.

And your grandmother is dead.

I was all *Holy crazy shit.*
That is some crazy-ass shit.

Now,
there are a few things
you need to know:

The reason why I'd hear through the grapevine
that this happened
is because
we don't talk to Uncle Bob
Mom's only sibling.

Bob came along quite by accident
after a few miscarriages
not long after Grandma and Grandpa Cooper
adopted my mother.

We always suspected
                    THAT
had made Bob special:
the natural-born one
who managed to survive.

                              Bob
liked to wait until after we'd arrived
to have a shower
then wander the rooms
in a towel not quite big enough
to fit around his waist.

Grandma would say, ROBERT,
stop parading around the house
and get dressed.

It was Uncle Bob who brought me
to watch the first *Star Wars* movie
at the Seaway Drive-in

and gave me his stack of 1950s
comics, then realized they were
worth something
and made me return them.

When I was growing up, I used to stay
with my grandparents a week at a time.
Once I brought my bicycle with me—
I had this BIG,

well, "BIG"—I was ten—
I had a fancy ten-speed
to replace my banana bike
whose long orange seat had separated
from its post
during my last ride with it.

Bob said, I'm going to help you
tune your new bike.
Bob was a mechanic.
He never really had a job,
only reasons
why he didn't have a job.
He kept getting fired from places
for his ATTITUDE.

My grandmother had financed a brand new
double-door garage in the back property
where Bob could do mechanic work
under the table.

So
we took my bike up there,
Bob laid out all the tools on a towel
and he showed me how to do things.

I was like, *Oh my god, Bob's actually
being nice to me.*

He didn't do things like this for me,

he preferred my sister,
and here he was
showing me
how to take things apart
and use this tool
                    and put this here
and put that there.

I took off the pedals and chain
and brakes and axle
and removed all the ball bearings.

When we were done
and I had cleaned everything
Bob stopped
looked at me
then looked at the pile of shit on the ground
and said, Okay,
now
put it back together.

I was like, *You didn't tell me*
that I needed to memorize
what came
from where.

We hadn't put parts down in any order
nor any recognizable system.

       Keep in mind
       I'm a ten-year-old sissy.

       I didn't know about bicycles.
       I didn't know anything about anything
       except Holly Hobbie, let's be honest.
So,
    I started to freak out.
I broke into a sweat. And squeaked,
I don't know how to do this.

Bob answered, That
is your first lesson then.
Pay attention.

And walked away.

The older you get the stranger
your childhood can seem.

My grandparents lived in a two-storey
wood-siding home, with an oil-burning furnace
the size of a dishwasher:
from its dark metal frame
ran a big black pipe
up the wall and across the ceiling.
                                    Grandpa would often
open a round door in the furnace
and throw in whatever paper
he wanted to eliminate
in the flames.

From a corner in their dining room
they'd slide away the armchair to reveal
a trap door
like a large panel in the carpeted floor

a set of stairs
leading to a basement
with stone walls and a dirt floor.

That house
was packed with things and things
inside things. A wood-burning oven
disconnected, turned into
a storage hutch.

Jars in the cupboard stuffed full
of dried elastics and plastic bread ties.

The second-floor mezzanine
had sloped ceilings on two sides
with one bedroom over here
and then another bedroom over there.

My grandparents slept in the first room.

In the
        not really the eaves
but in the slope
at the end of their bedroom
they stored even more shit.

At the end of their bed they would set up
a folding cot for me, where I slept
under the angle of the room,
next to all of this bric-a-brac.

I could look into the stacks
of boxes, chairs on top of chairs,
dressers and prams and draped sheets
over who knows what
like a little world I could climb in
and end up on the other side
of who knows where.

On the side table beside the bed
my grandmother had a black clock
painted like a Polish Easter egg, a
bed pan she used during the night
        (I remember the sound,
        actually,
        of her stream
        against the metal
        because the pitch dark
        teaches you to hear
        even better)
and a white dappled barn owl
under plastic
that her dad had shot through the eye
by luck, so it had been easy
to stuff.

If I slept in their bedroom, you would think
Bob must be in the second, but
that room was floor-to-ceiling
furniture.
                              Bob
slept on the landing. Tucked
under that slope, they'd installed
a single bed with a privacy screen
that covered only two-thirds of
his body, so you could see
his bare legs
when he was lying there.

Imagine you're a grown man
you don't have your own bedroom

for years, you sleep in the hallway
adjoining your parents' room.

This is the story—when I put all my cards
in the Magic Story Bag—I said to my husband,
        God, I hope I don't pick
        GRANDMA COOPER'S CORPSE anytime soon.

By coincidence, someone had told me,
        When you're picking your stories,
        you should REALLY choose someone you're talking to,
and I thought, *Maybe*
that's Grandma Cooper

but

I just don't wanna talk
to a dead person.

So, I decided I'd talk to Teddy,
the bear my grandma gave me
when I was a child.
        What's that, Teddy, you want to say hi?
        Ohhh, you can say hi.

Look, he's waving.

She gave me Teddy when I was a kid;
he was handmade by somebody in her neighbourhood.

When I got older my mom
put all my stuffed animals
to the curb in a big box.
That same day my grandmother visited
so she saw everything at the curb
and said, What's that?

Mom told her

and Grandma said, Well
you're not throwing these out.
And she took my favourite stuffed animal
and my sister's favourite, and she kept them
for a decade.

For Christmas one year, my grandmother
—Teddy was missing an arm—
my grandmother brought the teddy bear
back to the original maker,
twenty years later.
          [Michael waves bear's new arm.]
This is a teddy bear amputee.

My grandmother gave it back to me repaired
with this little note saying, you know,
I love you, you're great,
you're the best grandson ever.

So that's my Grandma Cooper.
I loved her unconditionally.

But Grandma was a little bit paranoid.
When her own mother died,
the family fought over the will.

My grandmother lived in the house next to her sister
my great-aunt Theresa
my entire life, and I never talked to her.
I wasn't allowed to.

One day I'd only said HELLO
and I got such
a talking-to.

My grandmother said,
         That woman
                  is
                  EVIL.
         And you are not to talk to her
         when you are on
                  MY
                  property.

         You are NEVER to talk to her AGAIN.

And then she went over to the fence
and she yelled, THERESA,
you old witch,
don't you be talking to my grandson
blah blah blah.

Throughout the course of my mom's life,
Grandma got rid of all of her family,
all of her side.

And throughout the course
of my life she got rid of
my grandfather's side of the family.
She cut people out one by one.

The circle got smaller
and smaller and smaller and suddenly
we were outside of it too.

She didn't trust us. She got suspicious.
She cut my sister out first and then
my mother, well, my mother
cut her out when Grandma cut my sister out.

I saw her for a little while
and talked to her on the phone occasionally
until I just couldn't
handle it, because ...

she lived with my uncle Bob.

Who got arrested.

> Or, I should say, my uncle Bob
> lived with her.

One year, Bob actually did leave the house.
Got a girlfriend, moved out.

Her name was Gabe.
She was wealthy.

My grandmother always said that
Gabe was dating Bob just to make
her rich father crazy.

They had so much money that Gabe
would ride and jump horses.
She was an equestrian.
Her parents had a grand house
with an in-ground pool.

I went in the pool, but
I never went in the house
which tells you something
about the kind of people they were.

Gabe dated my uncle for two years.
They lived together for one
in a tiny little bungalow
that Gabe's parents owned
just across the street.

My sister and I
when we were up visiting my grandparents
we would have an overnight with Uncle Bob
or an evening, which I guess gave
my grandparents a break, cuz,
you know, we were two kids.

Bob and Gabe had bought
a Doberman Pinscher
named Terra.
                   I'd met the dog
a couple of times before.

She was a snarler. She didn't like people
because
                she was my uncle Bob's dog
and
she'd been adopted as an adult from somebody
who'd used her as a guard dog
for a site engaged in
illegal activity.

                   Guarding was in her nature.
She was raised that way.

And I was. How old was I?
I must have been about eight
and my sister was ten.

Bob brought the two of us in
to his new place for the first time
and sat us on the couch

then he put Terra the dog
in front of our faces.

Dobermans sit tall.

                   Bob said,
You have to stay on that couch
and not move, until I introduce you to Terra
in our house. And if you move,
she's going to chew your face off.

And then he walked into the kitchen
to prepare supper with Gabe.

And I swear to god that dog
sat there inches away from our faces
baring her teeth.

Bob, every once in a while, from the kitchen,
would say, Terra, it's o-kay.

He couldn't see what she was doing.
He just heard her tone shift.

He left us there, it had to have been
I don't know, twenty, thirty minutes.

        Those minutes are still
        easily
        the longest of my life.

Bob liked to do all these things,
power games.

       Even as a young adult, I'd have
a hard time because I'd call to talk
to my grandmother
who was the great love
of my life as a child
                  and then I'd get Bob
he'd answer the phone
and I'd be just, *Unhhhh
I can't believe I have to go through
this again.*

Back when I was still on the inside
but my mom and sister were on
the outs
          I called my grandmother and said,
I'm going to come to town, and I'd like
to take you out for lunch. I thought maybe
we could go somewhere.
It would be nice to see you
out of the house.

She thought about it a little bit, and she said,
WELL, I just don't think
I'm going to be able to do that.
Why don't you just come here
and we'll have a visit.

Likely Grandma thought I wanted
to get her out of the house so that somebody
could come in while she was gone.

Grandma, I said, like,
Bob can stay in the house.
I just want to see you
without having to see him,
because he's not always nice to me.

And she was like, OH it'll be fine,
I'll just tell him. To be nice.

So,
I go see her.

I come in the door and there's my uncle
standing in the kitchen
the minute I walk in, and seeing me
for the first time in
two years or something
he says,
Do you vacuum?

Yeah, I know how to vacuum.

And he's all, Good, you can vacuum
your grandmother's house.

Dude, this is your house.
You live here.
Why can't you vacuum
your own fucking house
for your own fucking mother
who you don't pay rent to?
    But that was just in my head.

I vacuum.
   Then we have leftover
hamburgers and skillet-fried KD for dinner.
Through the whole meal
Bob is dominating the conversation
so my grandmother and I don't get to talk.

Bob tells me this story
of how he was driving to Ottawa last week
about a forty-minute drive
and it's only a two-lane highway for a bunch of it.

Some car was driving too slow;
tailgating
to speed him up
didn't work.

Then, there was a passing lane
and the Camry didn't move over.

                    At the second one
again he didn't pull over, so Bob
laid on his horn,
and went around the guy in the slow lane
            then
when the highway reverts
to single lanes
Bob slows his car down to nothing
and forces the other guy
to stop in behind him on the highway.

Bob goes into the back seat of his car
and, he says, he pulls out a tire iron

and walks up to the guy in the other car
and he shouts at his window,
            Oh you think
            you're really funny, right?

            That was a really good trick.
            Why don't you get out
            and I'll show you what funny is.
            I've got a few fucking tricks of my own.

So-ooo then,
my uncle proceeds to bad-mouth
my sister.

And I say, Look, I'm not gonna
stay here if you're gonna talk shit
about my sister.
I'm not going to engage
in any of this.
We can talk about other things.

And Bob, he's so

      you know, you grow up with somebody
who torments you, and you just become

            you turn into an adult
and it makes you sick to your stomach
to look at him

        to even just physically look
makes the anxiety run through you.

I remember staring at the table,
kind of dissociating

               unable to move,

thinking, *What the fuck*
am I gonna

how am I gonna

I don't know how to navigate this

I don't have the skills

And Bob, he's saying, Michael,
Look at me.
             Look at me.
Michael, look at me. Look me in the eyes.

Look me in the eyes.

And I,

I finally say, I'm not having
this conversation.
I don't even want
to look at you.

And my grandmother—
                            um

I'm

          while

while we were sitting there

I'd been looking at my grandmother

to see if she had bruises on her face or arms

          if she was abused in any way

because they'd been living alone
for quite a few years.
Her strength was declining.
Bob was obviously getting more dangerous.
I wanted to know if she was okay.

My grandmother had had this way
of controlling him.

She would talk with her lips
pulled so tight they appeared
curled over her teeth.

And she would say

[Michael demonstrates]

Robert, Robert, that's enough.
Stop it.
Right. Now.

And he would stop.
She used that same tone
for example, to force him
to put my ten-speed
back together.

And so she did. At the dinner table.

And he did.

And then it was reasonably civil
you know. I stayed another
twenty minutes
and that was that.

My last visit.
The last time
I ever saw my grandmother alive.

The last time I saw my uncle too.

You should know that my parents
didn't get along. They weren't the best
partners in the world.
They were good people, but
they weren't good partners.
Dad drank all the time. We were really poor.
Family life was stressful.

So we'd go visit my grandmother
for a much-needed break.
When we were young
my grandmother loved us best.

That's who my Grandma Cooper was
and that's why we hadn't heard from her
in ten years.

When we called my uncle Ted
to ask him what he knew
about Bob's arrest and his
alleged transportation
of Grandma's corpse

he didn't know anything.

So what do you do?
                      Well, we thought,
Bob got arrested, so we'll call the police.

Kemptville is pretty much a bedroom community.
Back then, it was probably 1,500 people.
It was very tiny. I don't know. Maybe 2,000.
That small.

So we call the police and we say,
I got this weird message from my uncle Ted
that my grandmother Jessie Cooper has died,
and my grandmother doesn't talk to us anymore
and she lives with my uncle Bob
and my uncle Bob is kind of a piece of work,
so I just want to check in with you and see,

> Did my Grandma Cooper actually die
> and was my uncle Bob arrested
> for transporting her corpse?

The cop was like, Okay,

> we know who Bob Cooper is.
> And this
> is what I'm allowed to tell you
> legally.
>
> He was arrested for stalking somebody.
> Criminal harassment.
>
> He wasn't arrested for transporting a corpse.
> I don't know anything about your grandmother's death.

I said something like, Oh,
that's weird.
> So what do we do now?

And the cop was really sweet. He said,
Well, if I were you, I would call the funeral home
because there's only one in town.

And I was like, Oh, that's smart.

I thanked him and hung up the phone.
I told my mom and sister.

Now, we couldn't call Bob,
he wouldn't answer the phone.

My grandfather had died twenty-three years before
and for all those years after his death
when you called and got the machine
it referenced his name.
> Bob and Grandma had
> recorded it this way
> recently, on purpose.

They recorded his name in there because
they didn't want to have their names
on their own telephone.

They were suspicious talking on the phone,
they thought their phones were bugged.

Anyways, so, we were going to call the funeral home
and my mom says,
I don't know if I want to do this.
This is really intense.

I don't know how
we decided I was going to do it, maybe
it's because I was home
and I rarely get to be present
for big life things like this

soooo ... I call the funeral home
and I get somebody on the phone
and I say, I heard that my grandmother
Jessie Cooper has died
and I just want to check in because I'm estranged
from my uncle and I haven't heard about it
and so I'm wondering if you know anything.

And they are like, Oh.

Oh, Jessie Cooper.

Okay. Give me a minute.
I have to talk to the director of the funeral home.

I say, Uhhhh, are you "going to talk to the director"
because that means you're going to hang up
and you're going to call my uncle?

Because he's kind of intense
and a bit craycray
and I'm afraid that, you know,
he's just going to tell you not to tell me anything.

And I'd really like to find out.

        And she says, Oh no,
I'm familiar with your uncle.

        Apparently, it's a catchphrase in Kemptville.
        I'm familiar with your uncle.

I'm familiar with your uncle and I'm just going
to talk to the director because
I need to know what I'm legally
allowed to tell you.

And I'm like, Okay.

And she hangs up the phone.

So here's the thing. While we're waiting
we talk about it
and my mom and I say the same thing.

You know, when we first heard that Bob
was transporting a corpse to the morgue,
we were like,
        That's so weird.
        I always thought
        he'd bury her
        in the dirt-floor basement.

We always thought
he'd just dig a grave
and throw her in.

Honest to god.
Both of us.

Yesterday when I called my mother
and my sister to say, Okay, I'm just giving you
a heads-up, in case you're watching my show
that, you know,
I'm going to talk about Grandma Cooper
and the whole death story

my mom gave me a list of things
she wanted to make sure I didn't forget:

When my grandfather died, Grandma and Bob didn't tell anybody except us. They didn't tell any of his extended family. Many live nearby. In fact, his niece used to live WITH them, for a decade, after her husband died in a farming accident, and they didn't even tell her. Muriel was like,

like, like

she was like his own daughter in a way, right? They'd taken her in.

By coincidence, her son showed up at the door the day before the ceremony. There was going to be a little service just in the living room of their house.

My grandmother asked him if WE had called him (we didn't have his number) implying that's why he'd come to their door. And he was like, No, it's just a coincidence. What's going on, I don't know what you're talking about.

And that's how he found out that his great-uncle had died.

They packed my grandfather into a pine box. Pine. Box. He was getting cremated wearing pajamas. No socks. They were going to just send him off and cremate him like that.

My mom was mortified so she went to some fabric store and bought a couple yards of satin to put underneath him.

Mom said, Look, I think we need to do something for Dad, like, he's just in a plain box. Mom, you can't just put him in there with nothing. So I bought him some fabric. And I want to get him a pillow. Like, where's his pillow?

And Grandma said, No no no, I'm not going to give you a pillow. But you know what? He loved Benji [their dog, who had died that year] he loved Benji, why don't you use the dog's pillow?

Mom was like, Are you kidding me?

No no no, he loved that dog. He would be happy to have that pillow.

So Mom brought the pillow to the funeral home or wherever they were going to burn his corpse. Grandpa Cooper's corpse. And she was really embarrassed because it was covered in fur. You know, where are you going to clean it? You get handed the pillow and away you go.

She showed up, and wasn't the funeral director the son of somebody she went to school with from grade one to thirteen.

She was so mortified, she made a point—I wrote it down—to tell me she was embarrassed.

The whole time that Grandpa was in the pine box, they were fixing this, that and the other thing. My uncle Bob, maybe the nicest thing he's ever done, he lifted Grandpa's head and put the pillow underneath the satin.

My grandmother was poking him in the pelvic area to see if they had taken his diaper off.

Bob had his camera at the funeral home. He was taking photographs. Standing on a chair, over top of his father's sockless body, going click
click click.

There.

Those are all the things that my mother wanted me to tell you about my Grandpa Cooper.

So the phone rings, and it's the funeral director
and Mom talks to him.

He says, Look, I know your brother.
Your mother passed away
in a hospital on such and such a date.

       We were in May, I think,
       yeah,
       this all happened in May.

She passed away, he says
in November.

Five months.

That's how long it takes for word
to travel round a community
of 3,000 people that somebody has died
when somebody else
is trying to keep the secret.

Just in case you're wondering
on the metrics for that.

She died in the Winchester Hospital, which was about
a half-hour drive away.

They always hated the Kemptville Hospital, so Bob
packed her in a car, and they went
to the Winchester Hospital

—where I was born.

She died peacefully from natural causes.

I'll tell you, we were so g.d. relieved by that.

She died in a hospital. Not at home.

She isn't under a pile of dirt in the basement.

     THAT
     is my biggest comfort.

Grandma's been dead
twelve or thirteen years now.
Nothing has been settled in the estate.
We're waiting for whatever
is going to happen to Bob.

Last winter I was in Kemptville and I drove by
the house to see what it looked like.

It was all shut up. All the doors were closed.

They'd had a massive snowstorm
that month. The drifts next to the doors
were three feet high.
                              There wasn't a single
                              trace in or out.
Neither of the doors had been opened
in weeks, the snow in the driveway
sat that high.
                    No footsteps.
No piles of snow anywhere.

I thought, *Is he dead*
in the house or something?

                              I got clever
went to the gas station
up the street and talked to the attendant.
He wanted to know if I was Bob's
social worker, and I was like,
No, but now I know he has a social worker,
which I didn't say out loud.

He said that Bob wasn't staying there
in the winter. The oil-burning stove
never got changed over and oil
was too dear.

Bob didn't have water in his house anymore
either, apparently.

                         I later heard from
my uncles on my dad's side
that one of Bob's neighbours
had come home early one day
and thought her youngest was in the bathroom
having a shower, when out walked Bob
          —who is not friends
          with any neighbour—
wrapped in a towel, dripping on her carpet.

The last time this attendant had seen him
Bob's face was burnt red
from the cold. He'd come into the gas station
to warm up.

                    So now he was somewhere
renting a room for the winter.

We haven't heard from Bob, obviously.

I shouldn't be surprised that
we never received a call even
when his mother was in the hospital
for that week before her death. We got no
tidy good-byes or making up no
hand-holding at the bedside no
opportunity to say thank you
for all the love you gave
when you were able.

                        Bob's

last lesson to me:

you can be haunted by memories
you never even got to have.

You Queer

Footage

In Grade 12 when I was just falling
for my first lover we borrowed our high school
video camera and bought a Canon
mini-DV tape.
              At first
we recorded each other in the tall grasses
off the Marleau Connector, its golden stalks
rubbing past the camera lens
until one of us
appears, long-haired, serious
about being an artist.

If he suggested it
    one PD-day afternoon alone
    in my parents' house
I was thinking parallel
when we removed our clothes
to shag on camera.

Watching it afterwards was less exciting
than the deed itself
which tells you we were teens
who were narcissistic
only to a point.

A Parallel Universe

In some other
parallel quantum town
life has given me
the opportunity to meet
Al Charbonneau
at the hardware store
so he can say, You know
what, sorry I called you
a cocksucker
in Ethics class.

     But
     am I
still my own person
who answers, Hey, no, look
that's all true: I've been
a cocksucker
this whole time. You
are not apologizing
for the right piece
of that action.

When I'm halfway up
that hammer aisle
would I hear him say behind me,
         Hunh,
like he finally
gets it, or is the world
no better than a punch line
no matter who
nor when
nor where?

How Loud Are Men

how loud are we
allowed to be
in each context
measuring our
gay situation like
a library hush

did we with high
pitched voices not
get shushed
ad nauseum like
Mme Lukenda
who didn't criticize
the student
who banged
my head on
the desk but me
for squawking

so distracted
by her insult
I didn't think
to note until
now that other
boy who
lowered
his hand
in silence

Where Men Were

a shot glass stubby
bottle buzz cut
CB dirty fingernail
moustache blotchy
beard morning stubble
darts finger whistle
wood pile shovel
lunch box chipped
tooth scar tiger
eye ring spark
plugs paycheque
home bar La-Z-Boy

Abusers

after my uncle reveals
the teen who abused

my father there is no
undoing imagining

said man and I
together, to have a tête

à tête and live with
the consequences

of whatever happens like
his attempted suicide

—that's mean
wishful thinking—

how could I
tread here and escape

causing harm when nobody
is that dumb anymore

let me argue
that doing nothing

is not self
preservation

even you, meaning me
in a past life

drunk in the park
without condoms even

you are dumb
to protect a body

we sure as fuck learn
early to exploit

The Cornwall Royals

My first job was selling raffle tickets
for the Royals' Fan Club draw
at halftime. I can still sing
that phrase the way our manager
taught me.

The gig gave me free entry
to all the hockey games, which should
have done more to help me
fit in at school, except none
of the boys watched Junior A
—their families couldn't afford
the tickets—and I didn't watch
the NHL cuz who could care
about the TV when the likes of
Hawerchuk, Crawford, and Gilmour
were on home ice.

My parents' seats were behind
the Royals' bench. My mother
was known for yelling
through most of the game
so loudly our own players
would turn and bark at her
to shut the fuck up, lady.

Oh boo hoo, she'd harp back.
If you can't take it, play better.

Honk

if you read books as a kid
because they were safe
places to have feelings

Queers Like Me

can't stay in
their small towns

I wish I could've

gotten a job
like Scott MacG

at the Farm Boy

or taught first
graders at Immaculate

Conception, celebrated

Canada Day in
Lamoureux Park

ignoring the green

goose shit all summer long
where the fags swap

blow jobs at night

along the water's
edge like every second

Monday vying for the meat

prize at bowling
I might see the boy

who touched me

before I was ready
grown into a man

which explains how

I spent years in the same
classroom & can't

remember his face

That's So Gay

imagine the rooms

inside the closeted boys

who got sexy with

other boys

other boys

who later

hung themselves

Future Perfect

They tried to make me
ashamed of the person
I would have become

but the medicine for that
was becoming the person
I became.

Falafel

When I moved from Cornwall
to Toronto my first friend at uni
Loralee
          laughed at me
for never having heard
of a falafel.

She described it as a burger
for vegetarians, only
in a flatbread
with chickpeas, whatever
they were, but neglected
to mention it came dressed
in a white sauce which looked
like a squeeze bottle of cum.

In my family we didn't eat
in restaurants
that weren't either
a chain or Canadian
Chinese.

Crabs, lobster, mussels,
oysters. Anything with a shell.
Indian, with its breads you break.
Even ribs, which you might not eat
with your fingers.
I'm never sure.

It's tzatziki, Loralee explained.

          Gesundheit, I replied.
I don't know what that is.

Sauce.
What's it made of?
Yoghurt.

I cocked my head and balked.
Nobody
puts yoghurt
on a hamburger.

Things I've Feared Include

the classics: fear itself, the dark, boys
and where they gather: locker rooms,
public toilets, urinals

sharks, sea monsters, giant squid,
open water, fire, snakes, most bugs,
spiderwebs, Dobermans, pit bulls,
Siamese cats

myself

cocaine and other hard drugs,
enclosed spaces cuz of concrete culverts
used as play tunnels at the end
of our schoolgrounds

gas, gas stations, propane,
drunks, gangs, guns, knives,
needles, hospitals

being gay, then being found out as gay,
being seen, new environments, new jobs,
applying for new jobs

strangers at parties, Americans,
basements, attics, some stairwells,
horror movies, what is behind
my shower curtain, under my bed,
in the closet, under the slats
of our veranda, the creek of floorboards,
ghosts, an exterior door
unlocked in the morning

heights, airplanes, scooters,
excessive speed

AIDS, HIV, barebacking, blood

Nazis, serial killers, sleeping pills,
the death of my husband, footsteps,
the climate crisis, the collapse of
California agriculture, bee deaths

syphilis, anal warts,
cheating, alcohol, suicide, my mother's screaming,
my father choking to death,
his amputated leg,
deaths of any kind

being thought a bad person,
being a bad person, my rage, losing control,
killing someone with my car, or a knife,
psychotic breaks, an aneurysm, cancer,
prostate cancer, my uncle Bob, bankruptcy,
being eaten alive, the mean little
voice in my head

A Recipe for a Queer Performance

goes something like this:

Ask the audience to write down
on a slim piece of paper
an embarrassing sexy time

then invite them to flip
to the reverse & record
what they gleaned.

Answers will be varied.

Sometimes the lessons are simple:
If you give a man road-head
and get eyeballed by a family, you learn
not to continue blow jobs
at a stoplight.

A friend catches you masturbating
to a Sears flyer. You might
if you're lucky
learn that you are not alone
in these feelings.

Maybe you call your lover
by their dad's name. Don't
bang dudes with hot dads.

If you walk in
on your parents
there is room
for shared humour.

Maybe some guy gags
giving you a blow job
& vomits all over. Learn
to ask your sex partner
how long it's been
since their last meal.

Some lessons are harder
to fathom. One must live them
to understand.

                    If
while fucking in front of a mirror
you collapse and temporarily
lose vision from an orgasm
—an ambulance is called—
this instructs us
to be careful with the ego.

Or say you're high, tripping out
while having relations
in a tent. Horses trot nearby
on a path and you think
the hooves are people
banging on the canvas
so holler,
                    Back off!
Find your *own* fun.
There are many insights
to be had here.

Some flubs are complicated.
If you return from a college trip and Dad
finds a penis extension in your bags
now you know he can't handle shit.

              Something wilder.
A vodka-infused birthday cake
licked out of your butt
demonstrates an ability
to try something new.

Or classic. You hook up with a guy
after the bar closes, both of you
madly making out
only to realize mid-sex that
you're against a window
with fifty people watching
from the street. Always
be aware of your surroundings.

Tried to kiss a girl at the dance?
Got headbutted in the nose?
Blood everywhere, but
if you bleed on her
and she sticks around
she's a keeper.

Stillness

My counsellor buddy John
took a professional upgrade
course on speaking
to the unconscious
through this trick
of resistance.

The description sounded
super woo—
                    you hold your arm
straight out at the shoulder
while the interlocutor
establishes a connection
to a hidden will
within you.

So, if John asks me a question
while applying pressure to try
to lower my arm
and the unconscious approves
my arm should drop despite
my conscious efforts

but if the secret self disapproves
the arm stays rigid. A game
of who owns this body?

Think of an ask, he says, something
you want to change.

Hm.
　　　I could tell him
I've spent my life jumping
out of bed the instant
I wake up, standing
before conscious, but only say,
　　Lying in bed in the morning!
　　I want the ability to lounge.

John asks his series of innocent
questions, and, sure enough
my arm is stone on every obvious no
and rubber on the yeses. We're docked
to my unconscious. He asks
if this deeper keeper is willing
to honour my request.
My arm drops quickly, well
out of my conscious control.

I didn't give it much thought
but two weeks later I realize—
you guessed it—I'd been lounging
in bed every morning since.

Years of calmer mornings
have come and gone and now
toasty in the sheets, I have time
to wonder

who is this other
unseen decision-maker
beneath my will, willing
my body to respond
to random suggestions
from my professional friend?

Will we ever meet?

What else am I
not responsible for
but have within
my care?

Doppelganger

A grad student tells me a man
on her exterior house-painting crew
cut his mail-order
wife into pieces while holidaying
at an all-inclusive.

He was detained at the hotel
when he tried to leave the building
carrying the body in a duffel bag identical
to those of a hockey team
who were checking in
just then.
              Watch out
for that one, her boss told her.
Don't get too friendly.

You could argue I'm no better
for hearing of the rapes
my students will confess
having suffered on campus

              which I can only hope
              are not by the hands
              of my other students

or complain how nobody tells you
when you're starting out
that teaching uni will involve
navigating a workshop in which
a nineteen-year-old
says she was beaten
by her mother with a stiletto
for refusing to turn tricks
with one of the two men
she brought home
to share.
        I'll give you
first pick, her mother coaxed.

To be honest, I wasn't sure I
was better off for knowing
these stories
           and now no thanks
to me, you know them too.

I've resolved we are caught
in this compulsion to repeat
stories so grisly as a kind
of talisman. If we hold
the information up
awareness may ward off
another's fate.

This employer
who'd been in jail as a young man
believed every convict
deserved a step up. He knew
what it was to struggle
after being released.
That
like the genius of Theron in *Monster*
measures our compassion
against the slow fail
of support systems

as much as it humanizes
any denial of our potential.

I carry the story of that young naked man
on the sidewalk whom a police officer helped
back into Jeffrey Dahmer's apartment,
Dahmer calmly making up an excuse
for why this teenage Laotian
with little English
was nude on the street
outside of his building. The cop
must not have retained
from his training
how we trust people
when they resemble us.

Everyday

I'm sure you are like me and have wasted too
many days feeling guilty for the waste.
Is a day tormenting oneself really a day
of nothing?
                    Go ahead, watch TV,
you might as well enjoy doing nothing
productive. You're resisting
hegemony! The capitalist
industrial complex.
                    Complex, sure.
Here is what isn't going to happen.
Why write when there are so many better people
making books. Ours haven't done anything.
Who cares? we all shout behind closed windows.
Days like this even masturbating feels like
a cheap date.
                    You are going through something.
You can't appreciate your own company.
Open the door, let the air in, slide on
sneakers. Grab a bottle of water.
Lock the house behind. Leave yourself
knowing you may never go back, not until
the sun has reminded you who this other
person is, the one who loves anyway.

Facebook

                                        the sun
                              must be on strike
                                like the posties

Last minute one-way ticket
to Ontario. I might be slow
to respond for a while.

Overheard Dad talking to palliative
care today: "I don't want to die.
                I can't say
                why I don't
                want to die,
                I just don't."

Hi guys survived
another heart attack they put in
4 stents to keep me alive.

I figured out why

this is the year of the leafs

Packing up Dad's apartment.
Yesterday he seemed clear
and sharp, then he told me
he was moving into my sister's
unfinished basement.

They would put in a lift. He's grasping
at make-believe

straws.

If you're the praying type, pray
he might find some peace.

I don't recommend packing up
your father's apartment
all by your lonesome. No siree.

NO HOCKEY AGAIN TONIGHT
WHAT TO DO SOMEONE HELP

I feel like I'm broadcasting
a pity party,

                but really, I'm okay.
Thank you, Therapy.

home from hospital again hi everyone

My bounce-back father
is getting stronger, again.

I feel like I'm walking in a dream
of another man's life. Everything is familiar,

but different. I've been away too long.
Nothing's changed but me.

Shame on whomever stole
my hospitalized father's cash
and Tim Horton cards
yesterday.

I hope you gag on that coffee.

MERRY CHRISTMAS EVERYONE
HAVE A GREAT TIME

I would like to request a day
without struggle. The problem
with a big heart is that it's just
so damn heavy.

Sometimes I think Facebook
is my whiny place.

This is a week of uncommon stresses.
Common ones too.
                        For ex.,
my tenure package is due
and my father is losing his leg.

My father is living

a horror story.

Texting Dad about the surgery
he might not survive. Life
can be very small and very big
all at once.

                              its an extremely
                    sad day in this country JACK
                       LAYTON has pssed away

Dad's full care team meets today
to discuss his options. For those asking,
he doesn't want the amputation, because odds
are against him surviving the surgery.

So today we look at what are best strategies,
what is in store, with a man whose foot
is rotting black.

REST
IN PEACE JACK MAY
THE LORD BE
WITH YOU

Flying to Ottawa for Dad's amputation.
After Dad's decision, the doctor
walked into the room and Dad
asked him, You got your knife sharpened?

HAPPY VALENTINES DAY

everyone if u have
someone to hold today
hold on for dear life

Sitting bedside, awaiting Dad's amputation.
The waiting is rolling through him
as terror.

HAPPY FATHERS DAY
TO ALL YOU
DADS OUT THERE

Dad made it through surgery,
and he's still high risk in ICU, but
we're getting closer. I'm glad I'm here.

There are no words for the pain he has.
I'm freaked out. And so behind
on work. I need everything
to stop moving for a while.

My father has a stump
and bouts of terrifying pain.
How does one do anything?

Dad tried mango today, for the first time.
He said, "I don't know what it is.
Is it a fruit or a vegetable or what?"

I showed him a photo on Google.
He's feeling better.

It's like visiting from Mars.

I don't usually post about
hard times
but I'm practicing being
more emotionally present and less
disembodied.

I would like to report
I need more in-person hugs.
I need permission to be sad.
And maybe a cuddle date
where I get to be really
freaking sloppy with the tears.

THANKS

EVERYONE
FOR THE BIRTHDAY
WISHES YOU FOLKS
ARE THE BEST

I'm sending out a big
THANK YOU
to all my loving friends.
My father is much more stable
although he has a rough journey ahead
with only one leg.

                                    i met my FACE Book friend
                    this morning for coffee what a beautiful
                                        easy going person

                                          im a lucky man
                                         to have met her

My father's infection is all gone!!
He's been in the wheel chair
twice this week, just days
after surgery.

He's my hero.

IM MOVING NEXT MONTH CARDINAL HERE I COME

Pneumonia,
just to make his life a soap opera.

Holding my breath.
Thinking of my too-tired sister.
Trying to mark essays.

my god its warm out

i can hardly wait

to see the SNOW

I'm living a blessed life. You know
it's been a damn hard year, but the love
of friends has bolstered me.

I won't want to live
2012 again, but I wouldn't
take it back either.

I want the riches
that this year has taught me.

My father texted the other day:
"Are you still upset
about the Twinkie plant closing?"

I think the smartass
is feeling better.

The last text from my father
was a crack about Twinkies.

He passed away without pain last night.
Ernest Alexander Michael Smith
Aug 7, 1949–Nov 28, 2012.

No flowers, please, though a donation
to a charity of your choice
is always a kindness paid forward.

I'm a bit emotionally barren,
with some singing and dancing
thrown in.

Eulogy written, photo photoshopped.

Doesn't seem real, but we collect
the ashes today.

That'll move us forward,
I suspect.

Final touches on the eulogy, some practice,
then to bed. And my friends are lovely.

Sounds like I could make money
writing eulogies.

The day went very well.
I'm twice as tired.

I've been wearing my father's
gold chain and cross,
which make it more obvious
to me that he's dead.

What I find most troubling
is trying to reconcile the notion
of the vastness of the universe
—the seemingly infinite—

with death as finite, as never again.

And I think, Of course
we have gods
to resolve this contradiction.

Family

At the Bar Mitzvah

for the son of my high school
boyfriend who came out as
trans after we broke up, her
mother-in-law told me I should
be flattered to be invited
to their brunch the next day
cuz she had wanted cousins
to come instead, and my hubby
and I were the only people
attending who weren't related

and I in my gracious queerness
I resisted informing her that
throughout the four years
her daughter-in-law and I
were a couple I had swallowed
enough of her DNA to be family.

Sam Hill

From rural Ohio, some town
I can't remember—Middleton or
Middlefield maybe—Grandma Cooper
would look at you
fiddling with something you shouldn't
and say, What
in Sam Hill are you doing?

Sam Hill is credited with establishing the American
highway system. He made his money in stocks
so he knew highways and capitalism
could be bedfellows.

                              Wikipedia tells us
Sam paid over one hundred thousand dollars
to build ten miles of experimental asphalts
to show the government what concrete
potential looks like.

When my therapist asks me
to imagine a safe place, I'm cuddled
in the back of Grandma's Chevy Nova,
its blue dash light making her face glow
as she takes the 138 from my home
to hers.

She sings a ditty without words like
a kind of scat, something you might imagine
from a farm family kitchen, *hi-dil-dee*
and *twiddly-doe*, never a tune I could recognize
but distinctly hers.

In my happiest mornings
I find myself in the shower sunlight
singing without lyrics.

The stretch of highway from my hometown of Cornwall
to Kemptville where my grandmother lived
passes through Finch where my father, Mike Smith,
spent a year in a boarding house I never visited.

I drove through once or twice, the town
really a corner where you turn from this highway
onto that, wondering in which of those buildings
my father might be. If only I'd known
what the future held I probably would have
told him I was passing by instead of wondering
would I see him by chance on the street,
and if I saw him could I tell from this distance
if he was sober and stop to say hi?

There are many places my father lived
which I never knew, addresses
I can't now find.

My mother likes to tell the story of how
she'd wanted to name me Aaron or Kyle but
Dad insisted his son bear his name
which she hated. She agreed on condition
they nickname me Micky, which stuck.

The only family who called me Michael
are the Coopers, who are all gone.

On a road trip to California
my husband and I stopped roadside
at the Mary Hill Museum, namesake
of the wife of the late Sam Hill who materialized
in a stairwell portrait between
the museum's floors.

There you are, I said aloud.

For a month or so afterwards
I told the story
with incredulity
of that man my grandmother celebrated

until I researched Sam via Google, which clarified
that highway magnate wasn't the same
                                        Sam Hill
carried in my grandmother's expression

which makes concrete how hard it is
to learn something new
about the dead
even if they're famous.

MarineLand

Evidence of the trip abounds
in photographs taken on matching

cameras gifted to my sister and me
by our grandmother. Each camera

came in a little orange plastic case
with a transparent lid, a square

flash which could easily be mistaken
for an ice cube, and, to stay on theme,

the camera itself about the dimensions
of a cold ice cream sandwich.

This was our big family vacation,
the only one we ever took, really,

a four-hours' drive from Cornwall
to Toronto, where we stayed with

friends of my parents who had moved
to the big city, Mississauga.

We crashed in their two-bedroom
high-rise on something like

the 27th floor. My first time hearing
that little voice which instructs you

to jump off a balcony. *Try it*.
At the time, Cornwall's tallest

building was no more than ten stories.
I'd never been higher up than two.

I might still have the sky blue and
yellow ballcap I bought with money

our grandparents gave us for the trip.
Here I am in a tan safari shirt

with fake badges stitched on, missing
a tooth. Next to me is a fawn

and next to the fawn, my sister.
You can likely tell even in this

blurry image that Leica hasn't any
eyelashes. She is just at the start

of twenty years of trichotillomania,
a fancy word for a simple problem

which left unceremoniously after
the birth of her second kid,

which, I feel compelled to record,
resembles the attitude my family took

to Grandma Smith being mostly
house-bound, which nobody

ever called agoraphobia, because
people without the means

to fix a problem often also ignore
its vocabulary.

The two memories that I have polished
best these forty years

are the massive wash of water
the orcas displaced

on all those seated
in the front rows of the arena,

a tidal wave of engineered seawater
leaping over glass walls, which

even at the time, felt like animal
vengeance;

                    and the second is standing
in a long line to get into the park,

too many hours in the sun, so I suffered
heatstroke. My mother brought me

to the flower bed to throw up,
only I fainted instead. Someone offered

aspirin. An employee came to see
if I was all right, then let us jump

the queue. Once inside the grounds,
my father joked how lucky they all were

to have brought me.
I was good for something.

1990

a young fag I never dreamed
I could be wore a flower-
print dress to convocation

the first person in his extended
family to university he ate
well most of the time he was

angry a lot and lonely despite
having a boyfriend he still has
today only differently

with fewer favours the world makes
you lonely when it tries
to convince you you don't

belong by the world
I mean straight people
that's a strategy right there

how they convince you
their language is yours too
my Grandma Cooper

was at said convocation her only
grandson graduating post
secondary in a metropolis

for our first time together
we went for supper
everything about being a fag

and having a grandmother was
weird in that time and place my
father was alive and in

attendance I wore a dress
because I couldn't imagine
myself in a suit

which felt like complicity
in a family
of millworkers suspicious

of any education
they didn't understand

You Were My First:

friend in Grade 7
Hungarian
person I knew who owned a piano,
     drum kit, guitar, flute, recorder even

kiss from a "boy"
and kiss with braces

blow job
road-head
penetration
fisting
poppers

(this list is disorderly)

first time:
at a cottage,
waterskiing
living together
in a gay bar
on a plane
in a twin engine too

caught by police while making out naked
trip to Europe
writing a song
on a unicycle
juggling

first gay play
musical
orchestra
opera

127

first time seeing: *The Outsiders*
Ferris Bueller's Day Off
Prince
Sinéad
Jane Siberry
Ani DiFranco
Lori Anderson

first heartbreak
first ex
trip to Paris
serenade
Jewish wedding
chosen family

A Dream Writes a Poem about a Moose

My husband rushes through the cabin door,
urgency in his voice. *Get your camera,*

go to the window. By the pond.
There's a moose.

A vision I have waited my lifetime
to witness. Moose. Funny as its name.

Big and fuzzy like a beanbag chair
covered in fur, then propped on sticks

she stands three feet from the pond
tentative as a preteen who doesn't

know we can see her, uncertain
what to do next. More cautious

than any of us would wish her to be.
Minutes pass in a choreography

towards drink. She lifts one leg forward,
an ear twitches to the side, a long

pause, then the ear, pause, maybe
a step, but no, a slow swing of

her jowly head, pause, twitch,
step, step, pause, twitch.

Lick the air. Two minutes weighing
the odds. Her drinking

is pedestrian by comparison.
When she turns, it takes less

than six seconds for her to disappear
in the bush.

My husband and I rented with a friend
this place in the woods for a self-made

writing retreat. We're all feeling
pandemic fatigue, world

weariness. He and I take a walk
around the pond hoping we might get lucky

to smell her if she lingers on the air.
His olfactory sense is as refined

as the word. For the short jaunt, we talk
about how I'm feeling weirdly insecure

about a stupid worry: maybe I've been oversharing
for wanting to read aloud each new poem

as it's drafted over the weekend.
Anything I do often feels like too much

about me.
Not long after, my cousin

sees my Instagram post and sends
a write-up from one of those

dreamy books about what it means
to see a moose:

> You can feel proud of your recent accomplishment
> and share it enthusiastically with others,
>
> not to be boastful or competitive
> but for the simple joy of sharing.

Weird, right?
Everyday magic.

To press the point, this poem
arrived later that afternoon

by way of a napping dream
in which I'd completed a poem

about the moose, but I'd had a good idea
for an edit, only, when I woke up

I couldn't remember the poem
written, just the edit.

Now I'm trying to write the poem
the edit belongs to.

> This is a time to explore
> new depths of awareness
>
> and be prepared for
> increasing sensitivities.

Okay, yes. I'm listening, O great
cheesy book of wonder.

       I'm not sure this helps because
I don't mean to glorify synchronicity

but just this weekend I finished a story
titled "The Neighbour" then

went to submit it to a particular magazine
I'd forgotten had themed issues, only to find

the current call was listed as
"Neighbours." Sometimes

the universe is so quick with coincidence
you have to believe

she's responsive.

Metaphor

the cupped palm
of my grandfather

in the garden
teaching me

to curl
my own

beneath
the raspberry

to make
my hand

a bowl

Aunt Debbie

                    was buried
on my wedding anniversary.

                    Her wedding
had an evening reception
I wasn't allowed to attend, stuck
in the Coopers' dining room, unable
to convince my parents I could stay
up past nine—I wasn't likely even five
        (I asked and
        my mother
        doesn't remember).

The first time
I remember staying over
at someone's house without
my parents
           was at Bobby and Debbie's,
maybe a couple years before
their own kids were born.

We watched a vampire movie, on TV
or VHS, which began with a man
with shaggy hair clawing his way
out of his grave. A terrible irony
for a poem, but true things hurt
a little more just for being so.

We weren't particularly close to family
being the ones who'd moved an hour away.
The five boys were drunks
beaten by their father. Debbie
married the youngest, which meant
she got the best one
                    —we all said—
cuz he had four buffers ahead of him
to grind down the axe of his father.

Which meant Bobby must be the least drunk.
The lesser drunk. Which makes me fear
for his life without Debbie. All of us
we buckle with grief, outwardly
or otherwise.

It was in Aunt Debbie's home
that I learned my father had been
sexually abused, which is a story
hard to keep to yourself

in the same way a poem's silence
tests the weight of things.

One might say she was best
known for her gorgeous stutter
      which I always thought
      made it okay
      for me to be vulnerable too
but Debbie was all eyes

a thick dark ring
enclosing a light crystal web
in golds and greens.
Trippy. Disconcerting.
Singular, she had the eyes
of herself.

Aunt Debbie often cocked a wide hip,
her hand resting there too
talking or listening like
she cared about everything
you had to say. Didn't matter
who. She was all in.

I know other things only family
can hold, which is another irony
that grows sharper
the more you think on it.

Pretending Sleep

On nights my grandparents drove
home to their bungalow
on Rideau Street, Kemptville, Ontario
with crickets scissoring their legs at every
stop sign the Nova met, wind whistling
to a tune my grandmother pulled
fresh from the air the dark
delivered to the curve
of her tongue
        I would feign
sleep for the feeling of my
grandfather's arms collecting
my body from the dog-haired
back seat.
       The warmth of his torso
matched mine. His evening stubble.
One hand beneath my backside and
the other along my spine.

       The pretend
of my eyelids lightly shut.
The crunch of gravel, five
paces over cement tiles
to the wooden deck, three steps up
and two more to the door, propped
open by my grandmother.

No lights in the house. Whispers
about where they'll put me, am
I still asleep, do they bother
with pajamas, here, leave his shoes
by the door.
                    Lit by the dark
the deep smell of leftover
ground beef and onions
in a cast iron pan, boiled icing
and vanilla cake.

He sails me in the ship of his arms
through the kitchen, the dining room,
down the narrow hall, past the large
wooden coat rack and the front door
sealed in old plastic.
                    We climb
the oak stairs for too long
to be believed, the sweetness
of that time between floors
made more so by the dread
of the last four paces
which deliver me
to the spare bed.

My body cold everywhere
my grandfather no longer is,
like a wisdom the body knows
of what the future does
and doesn't hold.

Braiding Sweetgrass

All weekend I've been reading Robin
Wall Kimmerer

who is teaching me
how we are raised

not to recognize the world
as family.

The other-than-human
is communicating, observation

as a form of listening.
Kimmerer calls it a grammar of animacy

we are taught not to know.
Which makes me a lot less self-conscious

about my habit of talking to, well,
everything.

Last month on a walk I chatted with
a pair of deer, a wide array of plants

in too many front yards, and
a squished banana

> *—why are you on the street?*
> *who left you here?—*

then that same evening I thought
I heard our human neighbours

in their garden, only it was just a sprinkler.
So did you say hi? my husband asked.

It reminds me of the end of *Room*
—the book, not the movie—

in which the narrator says good-bye
to his friend things like Spoon, and Room

herself. As much as I was impressed
with the mastery of that ending

signifying the end of his attachment
to a place of oppression

he couldn't fathom, I was also feeling
his loss of animacy.

Now I can point my husband
to Kimmerer

who validates
my attempts to befriend the world;

Nature not as an object
we do things to

but a subject
we are in a relationship with.

So. Hello, Rock. Hello, Pond.
Hello, Banana.

Hello, Moose.

Notes and Acknowledgements

Thanks to broke press and Clare Thiessen for publishing an earlier draft of "Grandma Cooper's Corpse." This poem is (almost) verbatim: the text is from two merged episodes of my storytelling show, *Have I Told You the One About*, which I performed live on YouTube, daily, for many months at the start of the pandemic. You can watch some at youtube.com/c/michaelvsmith71.

Everything in "A Recipe for a Queer Performance" is also verbatim, written by participants in a World AIDS Day performance for Kelowna's Living Positive Resource Centre, organized with Kim Kinakin. Which means, yes, those are all true.

The "Facebook" language is verbatim, caps and everything, from statuses written by my father and me over the course of his decline. The timelines aren't 1:1, if that detail isn't obvious.

If you like this sort of thing, the poem "Future Perfect" became the closing words to my first feature, the documentary *The Floating Man*. The central visual metaphor in that film arose out of my first Book*hug publication, the concrete poetry book *Body of Text*, composed with photographer David Ellingsen. Thanks to Book*hug for publishing our weird little visual art poems.

A version of "Facebook" first appeared as "My Father Died on Facebook," published by the Alternator Gallery, in a special publication, *Privacy*, curated by the wonderful Amy Modahl.

"Footage" was published in *Canadian Literature*.

"Every Day" and "That's So Gay" were published in *Riddle Fence*.

Thanks to friends who read some of these poems in their infancy, namely Colin Thomas, Ruth Daniell, Cole Mash, Erin Scott, Matt Rader, Erin Hiebert, and Kathryn Mockler. Thanks to the Inspired Word Café folks and their feedback sessions. Thanks to Book*hug, Hazel and Jay, who have always been the loveliest of humans.

What a joy to talk poetry with my editor Ben Ladouceur. Thank you for your keen insights, encouraging words, and considerate polish. I love your books.

Francis Langevin is as great a first reader as he is a partner. And my favourite person. No competition.

This book was mostly written on the traditional and unceded territory of the Syilx Okanagan People. I recognize that I am an uninvited guest. My gratitude is deeply felt. This land is gorgeous. It nourishes me.

About the Author

Michael V. Smith has published six previous books, which include three collections of poetry, a memoir, and two novels. Also an award-winning filmmaker, drag queen, and professor, Smith teaches at UBC Okanagan, in Kelowna, BC, where he lives with his brilliant husband.

Colophon

Manufactured as the first edition of
Queers Like Me
in the fall of 2023 by Book*hug Press

Edited for the press by Ben Ladouceur
Copy edited by Andrea Waters
Proofread by Charlene Chow
Design and typesetting by Gareth Lind, Lind Design
Cover illustration: istock.com/teddyandmia
Typeset in Neue Haas Grotesque, Rockwell Nova,
and Gelato Script

Printed in Canada

bookhugpress.ca